THE GENEROSITY PRACTICE BOOK

40 Days to Unstoppable

CHRISTINA FREI

Christina Frei/Christina Frei Enterprises LLC
Contact Information – www.christinafrei.com

Generosity Practice: 40 Days to Unstoppable/ Christina Frei —1st ed.
ISBN 978-0-578-95802-6

Images © New York Public Library, Boston Public Library, Ian Dooley, Liz Sanchez-Vegas, British Library, Birmingham Museums Trust, Hannah Morgan, Cody Hiscox, Europeana, via Unsplash

To my little loaf, Sammy,
a dog who models
the Generosity Practice
way better than I ever could

It all comes down to this:

what feels good

to offer to life today?

CHRISTINA FREI

I remember exactly where I was when I created this practice: in my parents' basement on a visit to Connecticut. Eyes closed in meditation, smelling the mildew, I visualized something a little different. Whatever I was doing opened something up and brought a hit of joy. Most of my anxiety evaporated. I did it again. Same thing happened. What was going on?

I started doing this "thing" regularly and everything started flowing, including opportunities, connections, and fun. It would take another thirteen years before I started sharing it with others. When I did, I heard the following:

- "This is energizing every time I do it."
- "I tap into a generosity in myself I fully enjoy (as opposed to being exhausted)."
- "I feel calm and grounded when I do this."
- "I'm better at focusing."
- "I'm able to let go and be surprised by life."
- "I'm no longer depressed and it has stabilized my mood."
- "I know I can create something out of nothing."
- "I enjoy people more. "
- "I can better discern whom I can and cannot help."
- "I am more confident in my decisions."
- "Although I'm introverted, I put myself out there more."

- "I'm more OK with being rejected."
- "I'm better at paying attention to details in every-day life, things I used to miss."
- "I trust my intuitive read more."
- "I can say 'no' to others without the drama."
- "I can practice compassion, but with boundaries."
- "I can better stand my ground."
- "I have more energy to devote to people."
- "I can feel good in myself AND serve others well."

This is why I teach it.

The Generosity Practice is EXTREMELY helpful, connecting and mood enhancing – seriously, no joke. I use it ALL THE TIME. It is this cool way of connecting to all of life and turning gratitude into a daily generous offering of spirit. Best part about it, it is easy and quick and the results are tangible.

CATHY WHELEHAN,
OWNER OF YOGA STUDIO, REDDING, CT

Self-Care is Not Enough:
Personal Sanctuary Meets Service

When you practice self-care, especially meditation, it typically feels peaceful and lovely while you do it, but when you move into your day, the rest of your life comes like a wallop to the face. It's tempting to spend all day in the yoga studio with your eyes closed. I get it.

The Generosity Practice takes all the good work you do in meditation/self-care and alchemizes it into fuel for you to get out and make a difference. It's where your personal sanctuary directly affects how you help people. It aligns your inner truth with the rest of your life. If you truly commit to this practice, you won't be able to get out there and make a difference fast enough. You won't need to keep safe in a cave.

With this practice, you attend to your own joy in relation to helping others. You take responsibility for all this. This is powerful when you tend to give too much away or you tend to be more reserved. This is generative and creative work, where you offer delightful things to the world just for the fun of it. This helps you come alive in your service to others without being an exhausted martyr. You will stand unwaveringly in the truth that nothing is better than thoughtfully serving others and contributing to betterment of the world. This makes you unstoppable.

The Origins

I had a beautiful life in the San Francisco Bay Area in the early 2000s, which included a great job, a dynamic spiritual community, and an ambitious choral group. My days were filled with helping tech companies understand their customers better, doing energy work so people could move forward in their lives, tackling the toughest choral music out there (hello, Poulenc's Figure Humaine!), and generally having fun.

Within a few months, the sands had shifted entirely. No job, politics at my spiritual home, and a decision to leave the choral group. With no money coming in and no sense of my career direction, I started having panic attacks. I stopped sleeping, developed allergies to 35+ foods, and was generally unable to function. In a moment of humility, I realized I needed my parents' help and I returned to Connecticut.

Eventually, I recovered my health and was working in marketing, doing real estate on the side. I joined a comedy improv troupe, studied the Founding Fathers enough to become an expert speaker for kids, wrote a book about them, and got on TV multiple times.

And then it happened again. All sources of income disappeared. The panic started rising. I stopped sleeping as well. I had two choices: to collapse into the pit of despair that I knew well which meant sacrificing my health. Or I could use a tool, the mindset tool I had stumbled upon in 2001 in my parents' basement. I knew this tool could get me out of any mess. Now it was a matter of using it.

I boarded a plane in Palm Springs to return east from Thanksgiving break. My panic made it difficult to breathe. When I sat down on the aisle, I decided it was time to lean into the tool I knew would bring me through. I didn't have a name for it then, but it still worked.

The core question is about what I'd like to offer to the world. As I flew above Nevada and Colorado, I kept my eyes closed, waiting for a visual answer to that question. I saw black tiles, piles of sticks, rocks, and other earthy objects. I didn't understand why it helped, but when I offered these gifts to the world in my imagination, I felt connected to everyone and my body calmed down. I kept giving out things without trying to make meaning out it all. The more I did this, the more a deep knowing started kicking in. As I gave without any expectation of getting anything back, I got calmer and trusted myself again. Plus, it was fun.

When I returned to the East Coast, I intuitively knew the three people I needed to talk to for work. Within a month, I had fulfilling, challenging, lucrative projects. The money was coming in and the work was unexpectedly satisfying. I was sleeping and the panic was gone. Crisis averted all due to one simple tool.

The impact was profound and quick, so I had to wonder – could I teach it? Would other people without the meditation and energy work background get it? Would they benefit from it?

I started teaching this to whomever was willing to try. A small group in a yoga studio, a non-profit office, individual sessions, larger workshops, and eventually two field studies across five countries. I asked folks to use the practice for 30 days and report back. I wanted to know how folks used it, what results did they got, and what insights they had.

To my pleasant surprise, people were really, truly getting it. They loved the creativity. They grew more confident, less anxious. They got better at making decisions and more. It became the path of my life to teach this thing. I knew this in my bones.

The field studies taught me two things: first, that people experienced the real results I mention at the beginning of this book.

Second, business owners in the study got striking results in their marketing and sales, since it made them unstoppable and jolly (seriously!). That led to my Innate Marketing Genius work, which is a story for another book. Suffice it to say, every one of my marketing clients learns the Generosity Practice before we do anything else. It gets them ready for anything, it gives them steadiness, and it fills them with inspiration to get out and connect.

Literally in just a few minutes
a day of getting more aligned
and focused, I've had a much
better sense of my priorities.
When I have multiple projects
going on during the week or
even during the day, I have
a better sense of what I need
to focus on and how to get
the results that I want or even
exceed that. It's been a huge
help for keeping my scattered
attention and energy focused
and to get done what I want
done the way I want it.
Thank you very much.

BEN POWERS

About This Program:

The official Generosity Practice asks you to step into the unknown and make certain choices. It's creative but can be daunting. In fact, it should be daunting since it's a healthy challenge. This program is designed to prepare you for that work. You will get practice creating/imagining, receiving guidance, discerning what works and what doesn't, and making decisions. By the end of this program, you will be able to pause, close your eyes for a few minutes, and tap into your unstoppably generous nature, which is your fuel for making a difference in the world. It will knock your socks off, if you let it.

You will be asked to come up with ideas, to reflect on things, and sit with your eyes closed as you conjure up all kinds of things in your mind's eye. You are invited to keep notes in this book, and there are specific questions for you to reflect on.

Time commitment: 10 minutes a day is recommended

Guided Audios:
You might find that guided audios help you focus, especially at first. You can find them here.
Bit.ly/generositypracticeaudios

The

40 Day

Program

Day 1
You, the Friendly Elf

On day 1, you get to play pretend. Put on your imaginary elf cap and long ears and pretend to be a friendly elf. This particular elf wanders around town giving things to people, gifts that make their faces light up. He has assigned himself the task of making people happy and he can't stop doing it, since it's so fun. That will be you for today.

Contemplate lovely gifts you would give to everyone in your neighborhood, if you could. They could include puppies, fresh-baked pie, flowers, or anything else. Come up with five ideas.

1. _____
   _____

2. _____
   _____

3. _____
   _____

4. _____
   _____

5. _____
   _____

Nice job on coming up with ideas.

Day 2

Surprise Gifts for Everyone

What if you could leave a gift on people's front entrance that would make their day? (You're still an elf today) People open their doors and there's a delightful gift waiting for them. Come up with five tangible gift ideas that you could physically leave them.

1. _____

_____

2. _____

_____

3. _____

_____

4. _____

_____

5. _____

_____

Nice job on your ideas, your
generosity of spirit, and your
willingness to try something new.

Day 3

A Gift for a Friend

Contemplate one of your good friends. What if you could give them a gift that would make their day? What would it be? Include some details.

A Tangible Gift

(a pile of money, a puppy, a trip to Europe):

An Intangible Gift

(grace, peace, humor):

Nice job on tuning in, discerning what they'd love to receive, and on exploring gifts.

Day 4

How Your Friend Would Respond

Here's an intuitive challenge. Take a moment and contemplate how much your friend from yesterday would appreciate your gift. Imagine giving it to them and pay attention to their response. What would they look like? Would they have tears? Would they hug you? Let this become vivid to you and experience the appreciation and impact.

What you noticed:

How it was to have that kind of impact:

Nice job on using your intuitive knowing and on being open to your impact.

Day 5

Someone Gives YOU a Gift

OK, let's turn the tables a little. What would YOU enjoy receiving? Let's say someone shows up at your doorstep with something and it makes your day. It's over-the-top wonderful. This does not have to be what everyone else thinks is fun and lovely. What would REALLY make your day? Describe it below.

Nice job on using your imagination, being willing to receive from others, and on welcoming some fun. Even if you don't get this particular thing in real life, it will inspire something doable.

Day 6

For a Person with Challenges

There's probably someone in your life that is experiencing some challenges.

Their name

Put your attention on them for a few moments and see if you get a sense of what they need right now. What might be really helpful to them, even if you can't offer it to them in real life?

This Gift is

Nice job on paying attention to what someone really needs, regardless about your opinions or feelings.

I have found that among

its other benefits,

giving liberates the soul

of the giver.

MAYA ANGELOU

29

Day 7
Offer the Gift

You know that gift from Day 6? What would it be like to offer it? I want you to spend some time seeing yourself giving the gift. It doesn't matter if you can actually do this in real life. This is your chance to meet their need and experience what that's like.

STEP 1. Picture the person.

STEP 2. Picture the gift or offering. If it's intangible, let it be a symbol or a feeling.

STEP 3. Picture yourself offering it them.

STEP 4. What did you notice? Make some notes on the following: How was it to offer them this gift? What was their response? What was it like to see them receive this gift?

What I noticed

Nice job on exploring
what it's like to offer

Someone exactly what they need,
even if practically speaking
it's not possible.

Day 8

What the Whole World Needs

STEP 1. You probably have a sense of one thing that would help the whole wide world. Peace, financial stability, ending hunger, the ability to listen to each other in true dialogue, or true values. If there were one thing that would move the world forward, what would it be?

STEP 2. What if you could actually offer this out to the world? Close your eyes and imagine this. Spend some time with this. Give yourself a chance to make a difference and let it spread and become real. You've got this!

So what was THAT like, you world-changer? Make some notes:

→

Day 9
Ideas for Going Big

This is your chance to blow past any limitations.
No holding back.

Yesterday, you offered something out to the world. Probably something big. What if there were no limits to what you could offer? You could offer a billion trees, delicious meals for all, the funds for great schools everywhere, cures for all kinds of things, hugs for every person suffering, enough love for all children, beautiful homes for millions, or even a simple ice cream cone for everyone. What would that be like?

Jot down five expansive, limitless, no-holds-barred things you could give out. These should excite you with possibility. What if???

1. _____

_____

2. _____

_____

3. _____

_____

4. _____

_____

5. _____

_____

Nice job on going for it.

You cannot receive

what you don't give.

Outflow determines inflow.

Whatever you think the world

is holding from you,

you already have,

but unless you allow it

to find you,

you won't even know

that you have it.

This includes abundance.

ECKHART TOLLE

Day 10

Offer a Limitless Gift

What if? What if? So often, we want to help out, but there are limitations in every direction. Yes, we'd like to let every child know they're loved, but how is THAT going to happen? This can bring a subtle, insidious resignation that saps us of our energy and vision. That's why it's so powerful to imagine what true impact, what huge gifts, what real forward movement might feel like. This takes you out of problem-solving-brain (which can be limiting) and into possibility-brain.

STEP 1. Pick one of your five ideas from yesterday.

My Limitless Gift for Today:

```
..........................................................
:                                                        :
:                                                        :
:                                                        :
:                                                        :
..........................................................
```

STEP 2. Visualize the gift until it's real. Notice details. What makes it unique and distinct? Do this until it feels real, which might take some time.

Details I noticed

STEP 3. Send it out: In your imagination, you have the capacity to offer this gift out to the world. How would you like to do that? You could beam it out, send it to the sky, have birds grab it and carry it off, or place it in a river and watch it go out to the world. Play with this.

How I sent it out:

Nice job on offering something limitless and amazing.

Day 11

Connect Connect Connect! All-of-Life

You have offered things out to certain people and to the wider world. What if you had a clear picture of this wider world, grace, everyone, a place where you felt connected to everything in a beautiful way? I call this All-of-Life. Every time you see yourself here, it brings you peace or joy or both.

Determining your All-of-Life place will make things easier to do this creative work. This way, you can connect easily with grace and wonder. Let's do this!

It might be....

A night sky

A quiet beach with seaweed and seagulls

A church, temple, or meditation spot

A mountaintop

A river

A quiet barn

An old university library

A forest clearing

Near an old chestnut tree

A well-appointed manor house with a view of mountains

An old castle

A desert that extends forever

It's where you feel humbled by life itself.

What are some places that might do the job?

Five Potential All-of-Life spots:

1. _____

2. _____

3. _____

4. _____

5. _____

Nice job on contemplating
spectacular places.

Day 12

All-of-Life: Choose a Place and Hang Out There

OK, time to give yourself a chance to experience and enjoy your All-of-Life location and make it yours.

STEP 1. Choose an All-of-Life place from your list yesterday. You can always change it later.

My All-of-Life spot:

....
:   :
:   :
:   :
:   :
:   :
:   :
....

STEP 2. Close your eyes and go there. Breathe. Be easy about it. This is your spot! It's the best, or it will be soon. Each time you go there, it will be easier to experience it.

STEP 3. Notice three details about this place that surprise you. Allow each one to bubble up unexpectedly. This is a fun adventure where your own imagination will show you new things. Woot woot!

Detail 1:

Detail 2:

Detail 3:

Nice job on going somewhere great
and letting it surprise you.

Day 13

What You Appreciate as a Gift

No matter how tough or nutty things are, there are things to appreciate about your life. All it takes is a moment to acknowledge them.

Anything you appreciate can be amplified when you turn around and share them with others. Shall we?

Five Things You Appreciate: What are five things you appreciate about your life? A particular relationship? A piece of art? Your family? Some food? Your work? List them.

1. _____

2. _____

3. _____

4. _____

5. _____

The Practice

STEP 1. Pick one of these gifts.

STEP 2. Imagine it until it's vividly real.

STEP 3. Connect to your All-of-Life place. Hang out there for a moment with your gift.

STEP 4. Then play with offering this gift. Try this it in your imagination. Offer this thing you appreciate to All-of-Life. See what happens.

What I noticed

Nice job on offering something you truly value in your own life.

"The most important decision we make is whether we believe we live in a friendly or a hostile universe."

ALBERT EINSTEIN

Day 14

Trusting All-of-Life

Even though this is an inner practice, you might be wondering if the world wants your gift. Maybe you're giving out a lot of French Fries, but people have decided to go paleo. Hey, no judgment.

The good news is that you can decide how smart your All-of-Life is. You can decide that whenever you give gifts, they are taken to where they are most needed and wanted. **You can decide that.**

Let's check in. On a scale of 1-10, how much do you trust your gifts go where they are most needed and wanted?

If you are lower than an 8, take a moment to connect to your All-of-Life place. Hang out there in your imagination. Contemplate what is needed for you to trust it a bit more. Let this percolate until something is revealed. You might see something visually appear or you'll get another type of insight. Your job is to put out the intention and wait for what happens.

What was revealed to me at my
All-of-Life place:

_____

_____

Nice job on working on your connection to All-of-Life. You guys really seem to be getting along. (!)

Day 15
Create Something Out of Nothing

You've worked your creative chops. So here is where you step off the cliff into your pure creative flow! You're getting closer to the official and mighty practice.

STEP 1. See yourself in your All-of-Life spot. It's getting easier, huh?

STEP 2. 5-Minute Contemplation - Consider what might be a nice thing to offer to All-of-Life today. Let this percolate and come to you. You might visualize something. An idea might come to you. You'll see what happens. Perhaps it will surprise you.

STEP 3. Offer this nice thing out to All-of-Life. Go for it! See what happens and what you experience. If you need to, focus on your gift until it feels real to you.

What I noticed

Nice job on creating
something out of nothing.

Day 16

Create Something Out of Nothing Again!

You did it once. Time to do it again. This is a pure creative space. It takes practice sometimes. When it's messy, chaotic, and filled with unknowns, that just means you're on the right track.

STEP 1. See yourself in your All-of-Life spot (take your time).

STEP 2. 5-Minute Contemplation - Consider what might be a nice thing to offer to All-of-Life today. Let this percolate and come to you. You might visualize something. An idea might come to you. Perhaps it will surprise you.

STEP 3. Offer this gift out to All-of-Life. Go for it! See what happens and what you experience. If you need to, focus on your gift until it feels real to you. And you might have a new way of offering it. No one is stopping you from hiring a whole bunch of sharply-dressed donkeys to do the job.

What I noticed

Nice job on generating
a new gift today.

Day 17

All-of-Life Upgrade

You've been hanging out at your All-of-Life spot. Nice work. This is your short-cut to grace

On a scale of 1-10, how connected to All-of-Life do you feel when you go to that place?

1 2 3 4 5 6 7 8 9 10

↑ Not connected at all   Fully connected ↑

If it's less than 8, it's time to upgrade. You could do better. What might have seemed like the right spot is not really working for you. That's OK! Instead, you might want to hang out...

* At the bottom of the ocean next to large, quiet fish

* In an ancient Greek temple

* In a magical castle of your favorite adventure novel

So if someone handed you a ticket to a fabulous All-of-Life spot, what would it say on the ticket? Give it some thought.

My preferred All-of-Life spot

Nice job on taking ownership
of your All-of-Life.

Day 18

This Better Be Good

One of the key ways to deepen this practice is to upgrade the quality of your gift. If you're going to offer something, it might as well be good. Really good.

Let your own enthusiasm build. Let this be an inner adventure where you don't have all the answers for a minute. Watch what happens.

STEP 1. See yourself in your All-of-Life spot (perhaps your new one).

STEP 2. 5-Minute Contemplation – You get to offer anything to the world. Really. Anything! If that were the case, what is a darn cool gift you would offer? Bunnies? Homemade spaghetti? Money? Flowers? A compassionate hug? Let this percolate and come to you. You might visualize something. An idea might come to you. You'll see what happens. Let it surprise you.

STEP 3. Offer this darn cool gift out to All-of-Life. See what happens and what you experience. If you need to, focus on your gift until it feels real to you. And you might have a new way of offering it. It might explode like fireworks across the world. Or not.

Make notes about your gift, how you gave it out, and what you noticed in yourself.

What I Noticed

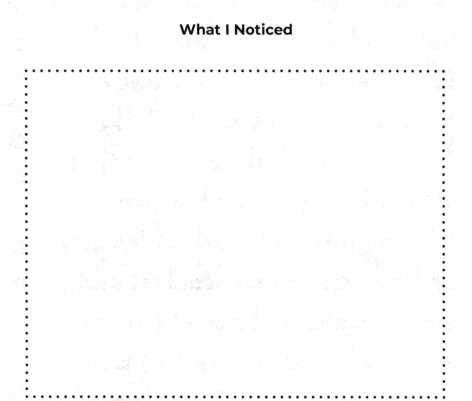

Nice job on making your gift pretty darn cool. Raise that bar!

I started the practice today
thinking I would give out something
light and fun and it turned into
something so different. I gave a
pen whose ink was made of the
finest organic dark chocolate that
wrote like velvet. The pen found
it's way into the hands of lawyers
and policeman and teachers and it
was enjoyable to be on the receiving
end of whatever documents were
signed in chocolate. This morphed
into planes skywriting message
of love and peace in the sky with
chocolate for all to see. It began
to rain chocolate in the shape of
hearts with little messages like

You would find on Valentines Day. These chocolate hearts fell on the terrorists and pierced their hardened hearts. These messages of Love, Peace, Hope, Joy, Life... changed them and they became like little children awakened and released from the grips of a terrible nightmare and they put down their guns and weapons. This was what seemed to be my longest GP and the most profound. This giving kind of freaked me out and at the same time gave me a sense of peace.

MARY BETH HAYES VITULLO

Day 19

Hot Air Balloons Because...

As you settle into this practice, you have probably noticed that you are directing this whole experience. Not only are you coming up with gifts, but you can also vary how you offer things. No one will stop you from hiring an elephant to take your gift out. Or covering it in chocolate before you offer it. Or creating a squall to lift your gift (s) into the sky and out into the wider world. Or bringing 1,000 hot air balloons to disperse it all. Or...you get the idea. Time to play.

STEP 1. Connect to All-of-Life

STEP 2. 5-Minute Contemplation – What is a cool gift you could offer to life today? Let this percolate and sneak up on you. You might visualize something. It will come to you. Just hang out, my friend.

STEP 3. Play with how you'd like to offer this bad boy. What would be a delightful way to send it out today? Does it involve goats? When you're ready, offer your gift out to All-of-Life.

What I noticed

Nice job on mixing it up a bit.

Day 20
The Trick of Surprising Yourself

Nice job on visualizing and offering. Time to play with **letting your gift appear in a surprise poof!** Ready for a little adventure? These are the best gifts!

STEP 1. Connect to All-of-Life

STEP 2. 5-Minute Contemplation – Take an intentional breath. Consider that there's a super-duper gift that you could offer, if you knew what it was. But you don't! And that's OK. So stare pensively out to All-of-Life as it cooks something up for you. If this is uncomfortable, you're on the right track. After all, you're letting go of control. Still breathing? Remember, there's a super-duper-fabulous gift that will appear. All you have to do is let it show up.

STEP 3. When you're ready, offer your gift out to All-of-Life as you see fit.

What I noticed

Nice job on being humble, on stepping into the unknown, and on letting something new come to you.

Keep your gift to yourself today. You can share about it tomorrow.

65

Day 21

The Official Practice

Here's what you've done so far:

* Come up with lots of ideas of gifts to offer

* Connected with something bigger than you

* Discerned what really is a good gift

* Focused your attention on this simple and powerful contemplation

* Experienced joyful generosity

* Visualized many things

* Let yourself be surprised

It's time to learn the main question of this practice:

What feels good to offer to life today?

This is the foundation of your daily practice. You ask this and get out of the way so the gift reveals itself to you.

Also, give this a full ten minutes in order to generate "the" gift.

STEP 1. Connect to All-of-Life

STEP 2. 10-Minute Contemplation – The Question: What feels good to offer to All-of-Life today?

Take a breath and contemplate what actually feels good as your gift today. You don't have to please anyone or prove anything. This is up to you. There's a gift that would be pretty darn fabulous to offer. You know this, even if you don't know what it is yet.

Be easy. Let it come. It's OK to feel lost and to get frustrated. That's the work. Keep going, my friend. Something is coming.

STEP 3. Offer your gift out to All-of-Life.

What I noticed

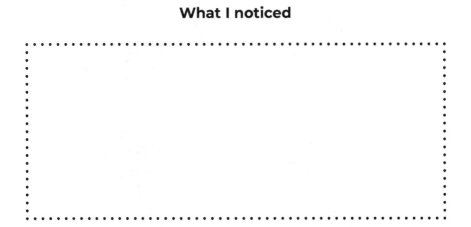

Nice job on waiting for a gorgeous gift and on doing the official daily practice.

The Official Question:

what feels good

to offer to life today?

Day 22

Take a Break and Chat with Yourself

Time for a check-in, a conversation between you and you.
Answer the following.

My overall experience when I offer things out...

....
:   :
:   :
:   :
:   :
:   :
....

What it's like at my All-of-Life spot is...

....
:   :
:   :
:   :
:   :
:   :
....

Since starting this work, I've noticed the following changes in myself...

I appreciate these things about the practice...

I'd like to get better at...

When I allow my gift to surprise me...

What I'd like to understand better is...

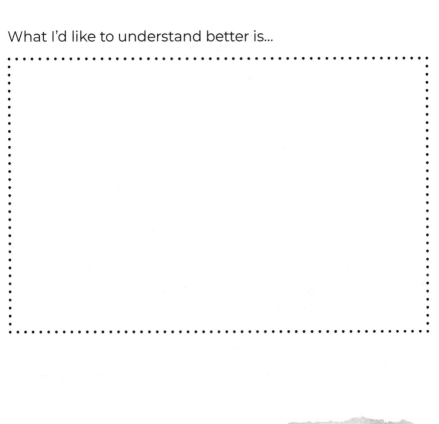

Day 23

Step into the Weird

You are an artist of this practice and artists take risks. They get weird and do things others wouldn't understand. Van Gogh is a great example of this. His art was considered odd and incomprehensible when he was alive, yet he was compelled to create it. Many artists have this story.

What if you didn't have to worry about being "out there"? What if you had permission to give any gift at all, even ones that might seem odd, messy, and slightly disturbing?

Edward Gorey created all kinds of illustrations that some consider dark while others find highly amusing (like me). He still created it all.

Name an artist you admire:

I have given out farting, stinking garbage trucks. I was in an environment that felt antiseptic to me, and these trucks made it safe to explore, make a mess, and try things. After offering them out, I did all kinds of creative projects.

So this time, you get to contemplate gifts that might seem slightly "off" to the wider world. It's something to explore. Start with five things.

5 Weird Things I Might Give Out:

1. _____

_____

2. _____

_____

3. _____

_____

4. _____

_____

5. _____

_____

Nice job on daring to be weird.

"Some days,

I give out blobs."

CHRISTINA FREI

The Generosity Practice is great! I love [the weird gifts] especially. I have given out the truth of anger and frustration as spikey rocks, mud-soaked trash -all rich compost elements for learning and growth. Yes, the truth is there is lots of anger and frustration within me and us and in the world around us!

It felt freeing and expansive to put that out there. It was my truth that I felt these things. Here "all of life" I know you do too. What's your truth? Let's not hide it. Of course, I know that whatever is the ripple of effect from my GP is out of my hands. I like that. I can give and release and trust.

MARY BARRETT

Day 24
Offering Weird

Time to give out a strange gift. You can either use one of your ideas from yesterday or go for something new. It's time to explore offering gifts that have your name on them and might cause people to stare with concern (always a good sign!).

STEP 1. Connect to All-of-Life

STEP 2. 10-Minute Contemplation – The Question:
What feels good to offer to All-of-Life today (even something messy, weird, or slightly disturbing)?

Take a breath and contemplate a gift you might offer, if you could offer anything, even something that smells like a swamp.

Feeling lost and all over the place is welcome. It means you're in the midst of a creative moment. Your gift will come.

STEP 3. Once you've "landed" your gift, it's time to offer it out to All-of-Life.

What I noticed

Nice job on offering weird things
and perhaps releasing the pressure
to be a perfect do-gooder.

One day, I gave out cement walls

for people to throw eggs at.

It felt so good to give this out.

I guess it was permission to release

some anger, whatever it was.

I noticed that all these people who

used to treat me like a little girl,

like my accountant and attorney,

now started listening and

respecting my requests.

I just didn't care what they

thought of me and my business

and it changed everything.

GABRIELA MOLINA
BUSINESS OWNER, BOLIVIA

Day 25

Making this Part of Your Life

Let's celebrate that you've been mastering three essential pieces of this practice.

Connecting to All-of-Life: You spend a few minutes a day connecting intentionally to a field of grace and life itself. This is the opposite of isolation, loneliness, and an "it's all about me" attitude.

Creating a Gift: This is pure creative genius, a new gift every day. You are creating something out of nothing for the express purpose of generosity. When you really pay attention to the details in your imagination, you sharpen your focusing skills and get better at observing your life open-eyed. As you create ideas out of thin air, you are also humbling yourself to a gift that surprises you. You are getting better at decisions on the true gift by asking yourself, "Is this it? Not quite. Is this it? Nope, try again..."

Offering the Gift: This is generosity. You are generating something in yourself and choosing to share that energetically with the wider world. You are practicing making the world a better place, even before any evidence is there. You are enjoying helping people and giving generosity a better reputation (rather than giving until you collapse).

This practice can be fuel for your life as a leader and change-maker. It is endlessly regenerating, generative, and generous.

Making This Part of Your Life

We all have our own ways of establishing new habits. Nonetheless, here are some ways to make this a daily practice.

* Choose a regular time of day. Many choose to do this when they wake up, others just before work starts. Find a time that works for you.

* Set a timer for ten minutes, close your eyes, and go. If you land your offering before, great. If you don't, consider using some ideas you've already written down in this book.

* Use the recordings.
  http://bit.ly/generositypracticeaudios

* Make this a spa moment. Where's a good spot for you to relax and focus? How about making some tea, lighting a candle, and getting out your favorite blanket?

* If a closed-eye practice doesn't fit your lifestyle, consider going to a café with a notebook and writing your practice.

If you do other meditative and/or breathing practices, the Generosity Practice folds in beautifully with other practices. So try integrating it.

I will make this part of daily life by doing the following:

Also,
Do the Generosity Practice

Notes on today's practice:

Nice job on determining how this could be
a regular part of your life.

Since you get more joy out of

giving joy to others,

you should put

a good deal of thought

in the happiness that

you are able to give.

ELEANOR ROOSEVELT

Day 26

Knock Your Own Socks Off

It's common that people give out nice gifts but don't experience a deep shift. The better your gift is, the bigger your personal results from this practice.

Here are some thoughts to help you improve your gift.

Consider that:

No one is holding you back from offering an incredible gift. You can decide to knock your own socks off.

It is common that people's offerings are so moving that they get tears from them.

When you get out of the way and allow an incredible gift to drop in, your gift can show you things about your purpose and it can give you deep sense of connection with humanity.

It will feel bigger than you, that you're not even in charge of this gift, that it's simply coming to you. That's a good sign.

The difference between a nice practice and a truly transformative practice is time, often a matter of minutes. Sitting patiently with an expectation of a great gift – that's what opens the door to something amazing.

Visual vs. Audio/Felt-Sense Gifts

There are wonderful feelings or sounds that can be given out. Compassion, encouragement, patience, and fortitude are beautiful gifts. So are certain sounds and pieces of music.

But visual gifts offer something that feelings or sounds (mostly) don't: they can surprise you. When we drift off to sleep and our mind starts generating images, our conscious mind lets go. Something else is going on there. It's the same with visual gifts. When something appears, often it's your higher self showing you something that might make no logical sense but that is absolutely the true gift for the moment. Visual gifts allow for truths to drop in unannounced.

Explore it and see for yourself.

This is all subjective (only you can know what a great gift is for you), but here are some very cool gifts:

* An unexpected check in the mail

* A winter bell that transports you to an untouched, snowy field

* A snuggly moment with a loved one

* Buying a stranger a latte

* Quiet chatter around a campfire

* That person you meet who is a breath of fresh air

*   The way a puppy is funny without even trying (and a kitten)

*   A monkey's freedom as he leaps through the forest

*   Delightful spookiness

*   A hidden sanctuary in nature

*   A roaring fire that makes faces at you

*   A love that can't be explained

*   Warm, spicy muffins

I have some thoughts on what would make my gifts even better:

Also,
Do the Generosity Practice

Notes on today's practice:

Nice job on being open to raising the bar.
It will make all the difference.

Day 27

A Wowza Gift

It's your day to raise the bar, which simply means hanging out until your hair is blown back by your gift. You will get lots of nice ideas. Keep going until you know in your bones that it's THE gift.

STEP 1. Connect to All-of-Life

STEP 2. 10-Minute Contemplation – The Question: **What feels good to offer to All-of-Life today?**

Give yourself the full ten minutes. Take a breath and hang out in your All-of-Life place. Stay open and curious as a gift reveals itself to you. Your job is to allow something to drop in and then decide if it's the one.

STEP 3. Offer it out to All-of-Life in whatever way you choose.

What I notice

Nice job on being patient and
raising the bar.

Today I gave a giggling baby

to the world. And boy,

did it feel GOOD! That baby was like

magic... He was flying all over

the world, and landing in

people's arms and laps and just

giggling hysterically

like there's no tomorrow.

DEB BEANY

What usually happens when you close your eyes
(in order).

Chaos

Nice ideas to give out

Some deep breaths and patience

A better idea for a gift

Discerning if this is the gift

Breathing and quiet and patience

THE gift

Day 28

Another Wowza Gift

You generated an incredible gift yesterday. Today is a new day and it's time to do the process again and blow your own hair back. This is how you keep things fresh and keep yourself interested. Your consistency is ninja. You are developing your joyful contribution and creative muscles each day.

STEP 1. Connect to All-of-Life

STEP 2. 10-Minute Contemplation – The Question: **What feels good to offer to All-of-Life today?**

Be easy. Stay open and curious as a gift reveals itself to you. Here it comes.

STEP 3. Offer it out to All-of-Life.

What I noticed

Nice job on opening even more to
the power of this work.

Day 29

Choose Your Spot

Let's say you've been doing the practice from a scenic river-bank. You love it there. But you really want to check out the Eiffel Tower. At this point, you're ready to mix up your location and go wherever you want. In fact, please go EXACTLY where you want to be in your mind's eye, including a stark desert in Morocco, a giant storm in the Caribbean, a Mayan temple, or a supermarket warehouse.

Get started with some prompts.

A place in nature I love:

An intriguing mode of transportation:

A great vacation place:

A moment in history I'd like to visit:

The kinds of animals that I'd enjoy a day with:

An exotic place:

A strange place:

A place where no one would expect me:

A style of home or building I enjoy:

Nice job on contemplating wonderful
places to go.

For me the connection happens in a few different places, all of them open spaces outdoors. I am never sure which it will be until I begin. Sometimes I am standing at the foot of an ancient chestnut tree, other times I am on the side of a mountain high above a lake and the connection

comes as I climb up the trail and

stairs and then sit in a shaft of

sunlight. Other times it is at dawn

in the desert under a crisp sky.

DERRIN CRAMER

Day 30

Choose Your Spot – In Your Practice

Even though you have a great All-of-Life location, you have the freedom to go wherever you want in your practice.

Including... a tall tower in a wizardry school, the top of Mount Everest, or in a gigantic warehouse in Nebraska.

Feel free to use an idea from yesterday's prompts, if that helps.

STEP 1. Ask yourself **"If I could be anywhere, where would I be?"** Watch what appears.

STEP 2. 10-Minute Contemplation – The Question: **What feels good to offer to All-of-Life today?**

STEP 3. Offer it out in a way that feels right.

What I noticed

Nice job on challenging your
creative mind even more and for
deepening your practice.

Day 31

Next on the Itinerary

There is a place with your name on it. It would be delightful to go there, even in your imagination. It might be a bit foggy to imagine it, but you'll get there. Let yourself be surprised by what bubbles up. It's as edgy as waiting for your gift to appear. What location is calling you today?

STEP 1. Ask yourself **"If I could be anywhere, where would I be?"** Watch what appears.

STEP 2. 10-Minute Contemplation – The Question: **What feels good to offer to All-of-Life today?**

STEP 3. Offer it out in a way that feels right to your location.

What I noticed

Nice job on going somewhere new and on
generating a gift out of nowhere.

My go-to is "peace".
It usually takes an
abstract form,
like white light or a
calming hum.

AMY FOLTZ

Day 32
The Pinch Hitters

When you contemplate all the gifts you've given out, one might stand out. This is a gift you could give out on any day and it would energize you.

This is your pinch hitter.

No matter what day it is, this gift always works for you. Mine is a cup of green tea. When I offer it to people, it gives me a sense of having a solid, respectful, open conversation. Works every time.

You could also call this re-gifting.

List some candidates for pinch hitters:

1. _____

2. _____

3. _____

Choose one and offer it out to All-of-Life.

What I noticed

Nice job on giving yourself
a break and letting this be easy.

Day 33:

Being Generous with Yourself

You are going to turn this practice on its head a bit by offering something to yourself. This is something a client suggested to me a couple years ago and it can be powerful. Instead of offering out a gift to All-of-Life, a friend, or a group, you offer a gift to yourself.

But not to your present self (although, of course that's an option).

You can invite a version of yourself that needs some attention and care. For example:

* The shy public speaker

* The disappointed lover

* The unrecognized child

* The failed writer

* The jealous friend

* The exhausted parent

Or any other version of you of any age and situation.

The Generosity Practice with a Version of You

STEP 1. Invite yourself forward. What version of you needs some care?

STEP 2. Tune in. How is that version of yourself doing? What might truly help them?

STEP 3. Take a moment to generate that offering. Notice the details. Let it become real.

STEP 4. Offer yourself the gift. See what happens.

I have found this closes an important loop of self-care, since no one really knows your needs like you do. This is you taking care of you in a gentle, attentive way.

What I noticed

Nice job on being honest and vulnerable.
And for taking such good care of you.

There are those who give

with joy, and that joy is

their reward.

KHALIL GIBRAN

Day 34

Therapy vs. Joy Creation

You might have noticed that you're giving out things that you yourself need. And then you shortcut to this by asking, "What do I need?" during your practice.

For example, let's say you're anxious about a work thing, and you ask yourself **"What do I need?"** and it's inner peace. So you give that out as a vibration. That's great. But if you asked yourself **"What feels good to offer to life today?"**, the answer might have been the way an elephant gazes at you and the sense that the animal is telling you something.

It's the difference between **a comfortable blanket and a magical possibility** that lifts you into the next thing. It's joy instead of coziness. It buoys instead of simply calms.

The strange thing is that when you go for the joy and magic by asking, "What feels good to offer to life today?", the answer is calming too. So go for the whole package.

This is about building your **joyful-giving muscle**, not simply doing **some self-care and therapy**.

The Generosity Practice

STEP 1. Ask yourself **"If I could be anywhere, where would I be?"** Watch what appears.

STEP 2. 10-Minute Contemplation – The Question: **What feels good to offer to All-of-Life today?**

STEP 3. Offer it out in a way that feels right.

What I noticed

Nice job on going for the magic
and the joy.

This is joy creation,

not self-care.

There's a difference.

CHRISTINA FREI

Day 35

Operate like Chinnamasta

The most powerful version of this practice is when you truly humble yourself and wait for "the one gift" to knock your socks off. This asks you to be patient, to expect great things, to shake things up, to not know the answers, to discern with self-honesty if something is the right gift, and to be willing to give it out. I have had people tell me they get tears regularly when they really focus on this. It can break you open in the best way.

Chinnamasta, a Hindu goddess who cuts off her own head and offers the blood from her head and body to those she serves, is a great archetype for this work. She demonstrates generosity but also sacrifices the ego (her head) that knows everything. You do this when you do the Generosity Practice. You step into the unknown just like any brave artist, so that you are more than a meditative Santa Claus. Waiting in humility and uncertainty is what brings the most powerful gifts. It never gets comfortable, my friend. It never should.

When you close your eyes, your mind will always give you nice ideas. Your job as a wise practitioner is to differentiate between nice ideas from your mind and the deeply powerful gifts from your higher self that evolve you and break you open.

The Generosity Practice like Chinnamasta

STEP 1. Ask yourself **"If I could be anywhere, where would I be?"** See where you go.

STEP 2. 10-Minute Contemplation – The Question: **What feels good to offer to All-of-Life today?**

STEP 3. Offer it out in a way that feels right.

What I noticed

Nice job on chopping off your head, metaphorically speaking.

Day 36

What version when?

Although there is a central practice, you've also learned variations on the theme. When do you use which version ?

Typically:
On most days, you want to do the Choose Your Spot practice where you wait for a great gift and offer it to All-of-Life.

When you are low energy:
Give **nice gifts from the friendly elf.** These are nice ideas for nice things you could give people. This is great for when you don't have the energy to go deep. Also, Pinch Hitters work well here.

When you feel scattered:
Focus on one person. If it's tough to focus and your attention is all over the place, choose one person and offer your gift to them. You can even generate your gift based on what they might need.

When you're playing small:
This is a great time for a limitless gift, where you go a little over the top with how impactful and big your gift could be.

When you want creative refreshment:
Bring on the weird, my friend. Nothing better.

When you feel blocked, vulnerable, or you sense there are inner wounds to address:
A gift to a version of yourself

STEP 1. Choose your version. Today's version:

> (empty box)

STEP 2. Do that version of the Generosity Practice

What I Noticed

> (empty box)

Nice job on discerning where you are today and what version of the practice fits.

Day 37

The Impact on Your Personal Life

When you do the Generosity Practice, you are generating a field of possibility. Today you'll get a chance to get ideas for your personal life. Start by doing the practice and then let it inspire insights in your personal life.

The Generosity Practice:

STEP 1. Ask yourself **"If I could be anywhere, where would I be?"** See where you go.

STEP 2. 10-Minute Contemplation – The Question: **What feels good to offer to All-of-Life today?**

STEP 3. Offer it out in a way that feels right.

Insights on your personal life:

Some ways I'd love to be generous to loved ones are...

Little ways I can be generous to strangers are...

I truly love helping people in the following way (s)...

What really matters to me right now is...

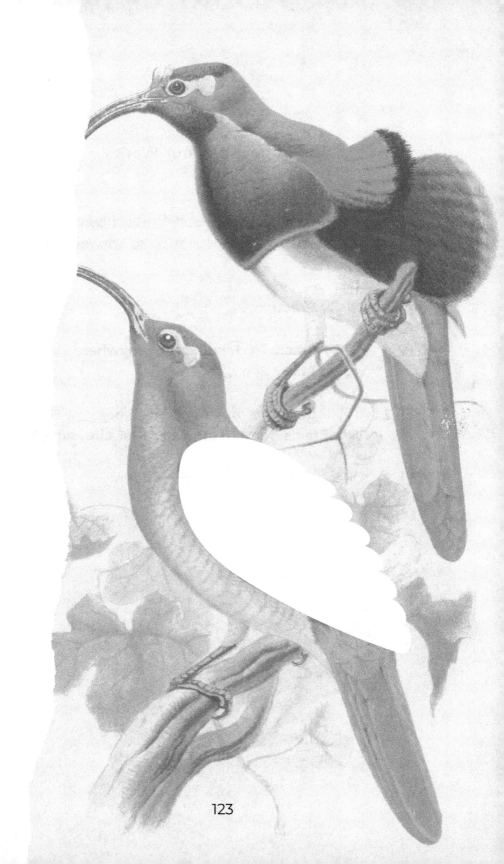

Day 38

The Impact on Your Work

What does this inspire in your work?   Start by doing the practice, and then use your inspiration to answers related to your work.

The Generosity Practice

STEP 1. Ask yourself **"If I could be anywhere, where would I be?"** See where you go.

STEP 2. 10-Minute Contemplation – The Question:
What feels good to offer to All-of-Life today?

STEP 3. Offer it out in a way that feels right.

Insights on your work.

What I need to focus on today in my work is...

An idea I might try in my work is...

One way I'd love to help those I serve is...

Other ideas and notes...

Day 39
Life Insights

Because doing this work expands your entire way of being, helping you be more present, have more energy, and have more compassion, reflect even more about how you want to live your life now. Integrate the beauty of this work into how you live and breathe. There is so much potential. Start with your practice and then answer the prompts.

The Generosity Practice

STEP 1. Ask yourself **"If I could be anywhere, where would I be?"** See where you go.

STEP 2. 10-Minute Contemplation – The Question: **What feels good to offer to All-of-Life today?**

STEP 3. Offer it out in a way that feels right.

Life Insights

I now have the energy to...

What I now know about my purpose is...

I want to bring this way-of-being into the following areas of my life... (career, creativity, family, health, relationships, vacation, etc.)

If more people did this, the world would change in these ways...

Now that I'm doing this practice, what I see if possible now is...

The kind of person I can see myself being now is...

Day 40

The Little Gifts Every Day

Let's bring it back to the beginning with little gifts. There are tiny moments and opportunities throughout your day to pause and make sacred, to infuse with a bit of joy and generosity. On this last day, contemplate the little ways you can have a better day, help others, and just connect in real life.

For example:

* Pause and smile at someone

* Close your eyes and breathe intentionally before a phone call

* Say "OK" in your mind towards someone who is upset

* Leave spare change in places

* Write a note of encouragement and leave it somewhere

* Notice a detail on a tree near you

The 5 Little Things I Can Do Today

1. _____

_____

2. _____

_____

3. _____

_____

4. _____

_____

5. _____

_____

The Generosity Practice

Take one of these into your practice.
Do all of these in your life today.

Acknowledgments

I have to start by thanking Laura McGowen for suggesting (insisting?) that it was time to write this book. I wasn't ready, but a couple months later I had my first draft and I was off to the races. Much appreciated.

Thank you to all my clients who have used this practice and helped me become a better teacher of this work.

I appreciate Michelle Stead for putting together the first digital version of this work. It helped me see what was possible.

Thank you to my early readers, Peyton Pugmire, Diane Delvecchio, Jennifer Henry, Andi Wolfgang, Kiki Kilburn, and Devorah Feinbloom. You took the time to review this work and offer constructive insights. It made a big difference.

Karin Rozell, thank you for reminding me that while this work can help all kinds of people, business owners are a great audience to serve. That's what I've done here.

Thank you to my brother, Patrick, for offering his Vermont home so I could write my first draft.

Thank you to all who use this practice to create a better world.

Thanks to my Norwich Terrier, Sammy, who always snuggles at my feet when I write and teach on Zoom.

And finally, thank you to Universal Intelligence for showing me this practice at all and for helping me share it as well. I am humbled by this path and am thankful it was given to me.

Generosity Practice Helpful Links

FAQs
Bit.ly/generositypracticefaq

I address people's questions and challenges about this work.

Guided Audio Recordings
Bit.ly/generositypracticeaudios

What's Next
Bit.ly/generositypracticecoaching

There is a laser-focused version of this work that you can apply to any area of your work and life. It requires a coach. This is a 6-step process I use with marketing clients, where they are challenged to define what they want and then link it to offering and being in service. It's magical and I use it with marketing clients to discover their One Voice.

Market this Way with Innate Marketing Genius
Harness the power of your innate generosity in your marketing message and strategy decisions to get great clients. Schedule a get-to-know-you session with me at www.innatemarketinggenius.com to get started.

About the Author

Christina Frei is a marketing consultant, author, and creator of the Generosity Practice mindset work and the Innate Marketing Genius tools and method. She helps brilliant, mission-based entrepreneurs look smart and get hired. In between, she chases her dog around with a stuffed animal snake, meditates on a pink couch, and obsesses over the perfect cup of green tea, all in a seaside town north of Boston.

Website: https://www.christinafrei.com

CPSIA information can be obtained
at www.ICGtesting.com
Printed in the USA
BVHW041946260821
615328BV00016B/1039